Red Voice

poems by

Nancy Takacs

Finishing Line Press
Georgetown, Kentucky

Red Voice

Copyright © 2016 by Nancy Takacs
ISBN 978-1-63534-075-4 First Edition
All rights reserved under International and Pan-American Copyright Conventions.
No part of this book may be reproduced in any manner whatsoever without written permission from the publisher, except in the case of brief quotations embodied in critical articles and reviews.

ACKNOWLEDGMENTS

I would like to thank Kate Kingston and Jan Minich for their generous insights on these poems.

Thanks to the editors of *Nimrod* for publishing "Echo and the Domestic," which was a semifinalist for the Pablo Neruda Prize.

Publisher: Leah Maines

Editor: Christen Kincaid

Cover Art: Serena Supplee, with permission of the Twin Rocks Trading Post, Bluff, Utah.

Author Photo: Ian C. Minich

Cover Design: Elizabeth Maines

Printed in the USA on acid-free paper.
Order online: www.finishinglinepress.com
also available on amazon.com

Author inquiries and mail orders:
Finishing Line Press
P. O. Box 1626
Georgetown, Kentucky 40324
U. S. A.

Table of Contents

Echo the River Guide 1
Echo at Dusk 3
Echo Swimming 4
Echo Accepting 5
Echo's Heart 6
Echo's Clothes 8
Echo Waking 9
Echo, Trees in Wind 10
Echo's Morning Walk 11
Echo in the Dark 12
Echo Thinking of Supper 13
Echo and the Domestic 14
Echo Looking in the Pond for a Minute 15
Echo, Fireflies 16
Echo Singing 17
Echo the Caterer 18
Echo Waiting 19
Echo Finding the Tree 20
Echo Leaving 21
Echo at the Mogollon Rim 22
Echo's Journal 24
Echo and the Dog 25
Echo Meets a Traveler 26
Echo Meets a Lover 28
Echo Speaks 29
Echo and the Word Red 30

in memory of my mother, Nellie Borowsky Takacs

Echo the River Guide

When I spoke words, they were
                awnings of balsam, bathing
the woods in a psychedelic show.

They were the apple orchard melting
                into the bleat of wild orchid,
the staccato razz of squirrels.

They were simple, carried out to the point of rapture,
                dropping seeds
to plant on the fig of my tongue.

I was the chord of the chrysalis,
                the pupa, and the wings. I was
the swarm, humming in the deepest well.

The words swirled like petals
                on a dark pool, spinning
to a tiny coast of fools' gold.

I needed a voice and the voice was there,
                never telling on the bear.
There were rolls of words, Life Savers
                splitting out of their silver.

There were words that roared like rapids,
                stung like nettles,
scenting the air with acres of sage.

They were fluorescent tents in a meadow,
                sleeping bags like Crayola cocoons.

They were pistachios and laughter,
                a Ouija board and eerie hums from us.

They were the orders I brayed when the raft
                headed for Skull Hole,
my crew paddling in unison to ride its lip
                in amethyst shadow.

They were the wild charts I sang
                to cross the shallow reef
when I took the kayak out alone.

Echo at Dusk

Now, I like the arm
    of an inlet, the lip
        of a crevasse.

I float near
    the turtle,
        the hush of his shell.

My head is phrased
    with lilies,
        myrtle.

My hair is husky
    with bluegill.

Once I could belt out
    Moonlight Cocktail
        or *Round Midnight*

Now, I'm the throaty mesh
    of doves
        and blackbirds.

Echo Swimming

My body is velocity,
a deep receiver.

I'm something
in pond and river,

bicker and blaze,
hurricane in chasm,

between each waterlily
shuttle and whorl.

Echo Accepting

There is a word dangling
like a star sapphire under the moon,
the one I was looking for
like the first bud of *trillium*,
the vibrancy of *tansy*.
There is forgiveness
in the well of *tepid*,
jazz in the seriousness
of *embezzle*, light snow
in the *squall* of forget-me-nots.
For some reason, *wolfish*
and *umlaut* swim in my stomach.
No word is counterfeit.
I feel it rise from
my knees to my esophagus,
each brim and perimeter,
each verge and neighbor,
each plank and mark,
each setback,
each threshold.

Echo's Heart

A bridge can be
a web, a chrysalis,
a tincture of elemi.

I like the eminence
of ice, the umbrage
of malice, of elegance.

I feel the venom of clouds,
the nudge of anemone
under my blood,

taste the fudge
in sandstone,
the open eye of cyme.

I eat the grudge
in love, paint
on eggshell.

~

Worry is a good thing,
not deciding, the sting.

Web of roots on a path,
alternative to wrath.

Bright caterpillar fur,
some way to demur.

Stark amaryllis lung,
pure stamen tongue.

Fretting green lights
of cooling nights.

The spider's last chase.
Resolute geese.

~

Cherry wood
and its hood, could—

the first robin,
gone then, gone sun—

a rush of rain,
insane, no brain—

eros,
ludos, morose—

forge, storge,
deep dark gorge—

the ice of pond,
small rink of sound—

Echo's Clothes

I learn to tie
the ah's of cotton
in my hair,

flutter an e
of please
down my arms,

run grains of g
through my fingers,

swirl f's of saffron
below my breasts,

crochet gold t's
in tansies
at my waist.

I want my skirt
to be the sound of lavender.

I want my shoes
to be unwritten,
unheard of,
unmade.

Echo Waking

The first sound is my slow breath,
the coming to, to the sounds
of phoebes, their *fee-bee* calls,
the drill of their wings
to the mud-nest
under my cavern,
making a bee-line
to my porch of granite.

Maybe I'll see him at the market,
talking to the man who sells
grass-fed beef, although he will only
buy onions without roots.

I think of him with basil, marjoram,
thyme in his hands. I might glimpse him
under the blue awning, bartering
for a peanut-butter cookie,
puttering over pottery
to choose a cup with orange glaze
for his nettle tea.

I'll be cooking fiddlehead ferns
tonight, their taste like
asparagus fogged, their halos
in my pan with a little garlic
and lemon, and maybe some
snips of basil, marjoram,
an echo of thyme.

The phoebes are in bed still,
the babies quiet and covered
by bodies, by wings.

The smell of ice is in the air.
I breathe into its crevasse.

Echo, Trees in Wind

Wild mint, chalcedony,
an edge of ebony,

vanilla and sienna burning
at the same-time

shadow, the turn of them
something that keeps to itself,

tattooed path of some life,
nothing like too much supper

but the center.

Echo's Morning Walk

Now I un-chasm him.
    Now I repeat the silky
        quiet of the pond I'm a piece of.

Now I have a curtain of beach, a cupola of ferns.
    Now I have
        a light-box of him.

Now I have envelope and carapace.
    The day begins with ice, lee,
        booby trap.

Echo in the Dark

It's true the hemlock of the evening got to me.
I should know better.
The abalone muscle, the healing light
of a painting called *Secret Glass*.
It's true the wrists of water lilies
made my breath uneven,
the fillet of water under them
billowing with algae.
It's true the weasel of the evening got to me.
It's true the waterfall
of the evening got to me. It's true
the Christ of the evening got to me.
It's true the whip-poor-will
comes each evening in a red voice
with a chocolate center.

Echo Thinking of Supper

Tonight it will be
carrots in saffron threads,
bulgur with basil,
a beet and apple salad.

I gather the whole day:
red peppers to juniper,
raspberries to vinegar,
cilantro to aspic.

Tonight, I'll marinate
a little eggplant in lime,
let it smoke over sage,
whisk some friendly

goat's milk with currants
and cinnamon in
a stone pocket. I'll
light my own tallow.

Echo and the Domestic

Give me the double chocolate cake,
its layers with a few burnt pecans,
their conversations about lures,
and whether they'll ever go
camping, or cut that oak
to build a table. Give me
a cigar from Costa Rica,
an old pink robe I can slip into,
give me the ruby ring on granite,
the tray of matched earrings,
the moldy bit of Swiss in the cheese drawer,
give me the musk of a bedroom,
the sadness of perky breasts,
the promise of prescriptions,
give me the girl texting in gym class,
the cocky school photo of the boy
with an overdose of facial jewelry.

Give me a shadow I can recognize,
which doesn't knock me back into the lake.

Give me the crow
to know what I feel and say it.

Give me any room, lavender with defiance.

Echo Looking in the Pond for a Minute

Somebody once told me
I have the long smile
of an afternoon river,

my shoulders
are the contour of mesa.

My mother
once said my neck—
without grace—wobbles
like a heron's.

I would love
to fly to New Mexico
to Georgia's home
in Abiquiu´—

her table made of planks,
supper of pinyon bread,
a vase with a loose-tongued lily,

the sweep of a dust devil,
one graceful bird
hovering.

Echo, Fireflies

Near the valley of wile,
    on this natural trestle,

I stand on my point,
    won't think of him

in this violet film,
    woodlark in hemlock,

the moon still in queue,
    that cut of justified,

unlike these bittersweet
    blinks, their bodies

a seaswell prickling
    my lank, umbos

of eloquence, who know
    my double wish.

Echo Singing

My voice is a broken arrow,
a cleat of harrow,
the tin of barrow,
the click of tarot,

the blood of fallow,
the heat of tallow,
the stone of shallow,
the heart of marrow,

the aim of knots,
the depth of pots,
a film of dots,
the rasp of shots.

My voice is the ruin of ice,
the skank of mice,
a hank of lice,
the news of dice.

Echo the Caterer

Watercress pesto.
Wild onion pate.

Tempura of fern
with milkweed dipping sauce.

He has a table.
He will answer the door if I bring him
a plate, or else he'll call out
leave it at the door.

He is not in exile, although
that is his favorite word.

His thoughts
are what he must do now
to preserve himself.

I change too often
for him, transforming
just today
from hazelnut salad
to cream over blackberries.

What reveals him
are dirty windows,
sun on nighshade,
clouds over mica.

Echo Waiting

I tap my foot.
After all, there are mosquitoes here,
and I have sautéed
little lobster mushrooms
for dinner in the grotto,
while he doesn't eat,
sitting in his lawn chair
out back. He doesn't
seem to hear the bullfrogs,
and I have eaten
the first spears of asparagus
and green tomatoes
with sage, basil pesto over quinoa
and the raspberry crisp.
I'm drunk on dandelion wine
while he looks and looks
at some simple shiny gear.

Echo Finding the Tree

I come upon the tree
in my wanderings,
the balance of flamingo,
the raised whorls of carapace,
the withered blossom.

I come upon the tree
when I look for a pillow,
want a turquoise sweatshirt
with a hood. I want
the skin of laughter.

I show him lives of wolves,
their loved footprint, their
nurtured calendars, then
the licenses issued to kill.

I show him the lives of
polar bears, veiled
by warmth, alone,
on ice floes, starved.

Echo Leaving

He is a leaf over afghan,
tongue minted
by Sleepytime, his rose
buttered by rain,
the firepit of him dazzled
by bells, not birdhouse,
wanderer between
hummingbirds,
looking for a shell
to dazzle, a fishboil
where someone
falls into the fire.
He looks for coats
of sin, burrows
of muscle, a porch
of adolescence.
He is the Atlas
of the World,
a coroner in the Byzantine,
a butterfly of flaws,
ribbon of worry beads,
cheek of carnelian,
immortal texture,
custom dark floor,
paraphernalia of sunshine,
shelf of wild rose
on a desert cliff,
hem of crisis.

Echo at the Mogollon Rim

I climb a mesa where I cannot go another step.
There are men on horseback, leading
calm palominos into the fretted
lips of canyon, the failure of wash.

My feet articulate,
my vertebrae haven't lost
their streams and cress.

I go to the very tip,
let my body feel,
my very strands
with their fragrance
of crushed trillium—
this ledge before vastness.

I want to catch quartz
after rain, slip down
the cliff's patina, hike
over boulders, geodes,
flashflood through
the throat of arroyo.

I am not afraid of fog
or the days that ring
with crow song. I am not afraid
between the ruddy mushrooms
and lichen like sprays
of gunshot set in all the colors of citrus.

I don't fear the violet before the sun goes down,
the remembrance of voice, or vagrant
paintbrush and candy tuft, yellow
blossoms of the prickly pear,
the fine last ribs of a muledeer
in the triage of dark sage.

I am looking for something slipping
across the valley of water-fallen
sandstone, granite caches
that have billowed here
a thousand years ago,
beige and crushed, dresses of stones,

veils of stones. I am looking for
the animal that will always follow me:
One thread for the needle,
one love for the heart.

Echo's Journal

The words are in my arm today, my right arm
that waves the gnats away, the vertigo
of hummingbirds,
the tattoo of fern,
bird-song like a celadon bowl.

The words are no longer on the threshold
of esophagus, the zenith
of my throat, the pen of my mouth,
the berm of my lips.

They are on the mist of my tonsils,
un-corralling from the roof
of my mouth, the mantle
of my tongue, the frontier
of my tongue.

The words are a vinaigrette
in my fingers, fragrant spills
over margins, basil
grazes in notebook,
gold nasturtiums over kale.

Echo and the Dog

His muzzle stays in my hands.
His eyes don't seem hungry.
His ribs are the ribs
of a canoe, his shoulders
rafters that shine under
his sleek dark.

He's an elm of gentle,
a swarm of bravery.
He looks at my handful
of hickory nuts. He turns
his head back to me,
teeth hidden, as I
edge off his burrs.

And then I know
he has to go with his
body, his need beyond
what I have today:
a bowl of chard
and sunflowers,
my last goat cheese
on a shred of bread.

He has to leave
what I want—touch,
this shelter. This animal
I would cook for,
who points a squirrel
and leaps in the blueberries.

He slips back for a nap,
then paddles in sun
to the other side of the river,
wags back at nightfall.

Echo Meets a Traveler

She keeps my tongue
in its wooden vase,
my head to her rhythm.
She says, *How do you keep yourself
so well? This is a cool cave, your
chickadees here in the hemlocks.
How many hours did it take you
to pick all this chamomile?
I love your tea. So fresh, so bitter.
Do you have butter, honey?
I'm going to the Utah desert,
to find dinosaur bones.
I've joined an excavation team,
people in a town there hiking out
once a week, to find a claw
or some teeth. Thank you
for these thimbleberries. I've
never had them before, so tart,
so bright red. Do you have cream?
What do you do all day? I know
you're mute, so don't mind me.
Just gesture with your hands,
or better yet, here, write it down
on this sticky note. Your hair
is so beautiful, so dark, and clean.
Do you have a mother? Do you
not write? Can I stay overnight
here? My bag goes down to
five below. I have some crackers
we can share, Top Ramen,
on your fire. Do you know
that the road is so close?*

You could walk to the store
in a day and buy some kidney beans
to put into that old pot
instead of those weeds—
are those dandelion greens
in this soup we're eating?

~

Are you making fun
of me now? You could talk
all along…

so close, that old pot,
in this soup we're eating?
of me now? all along…
all along…

Echo Meets a Lover

One day in Dark Canyon
he binds larkspur and aster.
He weaves the desert's stems and blossoms
to remember what is dying,
or already dead.

He has nimbled the wash
filled with deer bones, serviceberry,
beard-tongue, black medick. He ties
a paisley scarf on his head, loses the one
paper clip in his back pocket, folds
a blue page to preserve his thoughts.

He brings me news of eye-stinging air,
inversions over valleys. I think
this moment is the key. I show him
how to make chicha to whisk
away his sadness. He says
he will not speak until
it improves on silence.

Echo Speaks

I say *Peony*,
then *Pistil*,
for those new stars
I see in a *Smithsonian*
at the Tucson bus station.

I say to a young woman
with a 3-year-old boy:
Where are *you* going?

I am leaving
the scent of greasewood
this valley of news,
golf courses
like a charm bracelet.

I leave all the streets
of ocotillo and mesquite,
lucky to ride alone
with a bag of plums.

I say *bicker* and *blaze,*
shuttle and *whorl,*
hurricane and *whitewater.*

Echo and the Word Red

I am in for winter.

I take long breaths
to capture
crimson,
vermilion,

hold each
as if to warm,
then release

the last moth,
ruby-winged.

From a hemlock,
I hang bittersweet,

I wake up in darkness
to the copper star.

I wake up in scarlet.

Fingering a flaming
leaf, I feel
a supple spine.

Nancy Takacs is the winner of the 2016 Juniper Prize for her book *The Worrier*. Her book *Blue Patina* won the 2016 15 Bytes Book Award for Poetry. Other books include *Pale Blue Wings, Preserves, Juniper,* and *Wild Animals*. A former wilderness studies and creative writing professor at the College of Eastern Utah, she is the recipient of the Sherwin W. Howard Poetry Award from *Weber: The Contemporary West,* several writing awards from the Utah Arts Council, and the Nation/Discovery Award. She lives with her husband Jan Minich, in Wellington, Utah.

www.ingramcontent.com/pod-product-compliance
Lightning Source LLC
LaVergne TN
LVHW041508070426
835507LV00012B/1406